Wolves

Wolves

Michael George

THE CHILD'S WORLD®, INC.

Library of Congress Cataloging-in-Publication Data
George, Michael, 1964–
Wolves / by Michael George.
p.   cm.
Includes index.
Summary: Describes the physical characteristics,
behavior, habitat, and life cycle of wolves.
ISBN 1-56766-584-5 (lib. bdg. : alk paper)
1. Wolves—Juvenile literature.
[1. Wolves.]   I. Title.
QL737.C22G47   1999
599.773—dc21   98-36871
CIP
AC

Photo Credits

ANIMALS ANIMALS © Henry Ausloos: 15
© Art Wolfe/Tony Stone Images: 13
© 1996 Bruce Montagne/Dembinsky Photo Assoc. Inc.: 6
© 1994 Carl R. Sams, II/Dembinsky Photo Assoc. Inc.: 24
© Daniel J. Cox/Natural Exposures, Inc.: cover, 2, 9, 19, 20, 23, 26, 29
© 1997 Jim Roetzel/Dembinsky Photo Assoc. Inc.: 30
© 1996 Lynn M. Stone: 16
© Tim Davis, The National Audubon Society Collection/Photo Researchers: 10

On the cover...

Front cover: This *gray wolf* is looking for signs of danger.
Page 2: This gray wolf is hiding in a forest near the Rocky Mountains.

Table of Contents

Are you afraid of the big, bad wolf? If so, you are not alone. Many people think that wolves are mean, evil creatures. Some people think wolves like to eat humans, just like in the story, "Little Red Riding Hood." In real life, however, wolves are very different from the animals in the stories we've heard.

What Do Wolves Look Like?

Wolves look like big dogs. A large male wolf can be three feet tall and over six feet long. He can weigh more than 100 pounds, too. Wolves have pointed ears and bushy tails. They have round eyes and padded feet, just like tame dogs.

Although wolves look like dogs, they cannot be kept as pets. Wolves are wild animals. They do not like to be kept in cages or fed from bowls. They prefer to roam free and hunt for their own food.

This adult wolf is standing outside its den. ⇒

Are There Different Kinds of Wolves?

There are many different kinds of wolves all over the world. One type of wolf that lives in North America is the *red wolf.* Red wolves are very small and very rare. In fact, there are so few red wolves left in the wild that they are **endangered.** When an animal is endangered, it is in danger of dying out.

Other wolves are more numerous and are not endangered. The *Mexican wolf* is small and dark in color. It lives in warmer, southern areas. The *gray wolf* is the most common type of wolf. It lives wherever there is enough food. Gray wolves are also called *timber wolves.* They live in mountainous areas, wetlands, forests, and open plains.

⟵ *Red wolves* like this one get their name from their red fur.

Despite their name, gray wolves can be almost any color. Most often they are shades of black, gray, or brown. Some gray wolves that live in the Far North are pure white. The color of a wolf's fur blends in with its surroundings. This protective coloring is called **camouflage.** Camouflage helps the wolves hide from danger and sneak up on their food.

This gray wolf blends in well with its surroundings. ⇒

Do Wolves Live Alone?

Most wolves live in groups called **packs.** Wolf packs vary in size. Some packs have only one male and one female. Large packs might have as many as 36 wolves. Usually there are fewer than 10 wolves in a pack.

Each wolf pack has one leader, called the **alpha.** The alpha is usually the oldest male. He may be the biggest wolf in the pack. However, even a small wolf can be the alpha if he's smart and brave.

These gray wolves live in a forest in Poland. ⇒

A wolf pack is really just a family of wolves. The alpha and his mate are the father and mother. Their babies, or **pups,** are the youngest members of the pack. The other wolves are brothers, sisters, or other close relatives.

The members of a wolf family are very close friends. They play together and nuzzle each other. The older wolves help to raise the young. They act as babysitters, teachers, and playmates.

How Do Wolves Communicate?

Although wolves cannot talk like people, they do communicate. The alpha howls when he wants the family to come together. Wolves whimper to greet each other. They also whine when they are sad. A growl means "stay away" or "behave!" A bark tells the other wolves that something is wrong. Sometimes a family of wolves will howl together just for the fun of it!

This gray wolf is howling in a Montana forest. ⇒

Another way wolves show how they are feeling is with their bodies. A high, wagging tail is a sign that a wolf is happy. When a wolf keeps its body low and its tail between its legs, it is scared. An angry wolf flattens its ears and shows its teeth. By watching how other wolves in the pack move their bodies, wolves can tell how the others are feeling.

What Do Wolves Eat?

Wolves are **predators,** or hunters. When they get hungry, the whole pack sets out to find an animal to eat. Wolves like many different kinds of food. They prefer to eat large, plant-eating animals such as deer, mountain sheep, and reindeer. They also like moose, elk, and buffalo. If food is hard to find, they will eat rabbits, birds, and even mice.

This wolf is feeding on a dead deer. ⇒

People used to think that wolves killed animals just for fun. However, wolves kill only the animals they need to eat. Most of the time, wolves hunt weak, old, or sick animals. When the wolves eat the old and sick animals, they help keep the other animals healthy. That's because with fewer weak animals, there is more food and space for the healthy ones and their babies.

⇐ These hungry wolves have killed a sick deer.

How Do Wolves Hunt?

A wolf pack does not always just sit around and have fun. The members also work together to capture food. One wolf is strong, but a pack of wolves is much stronger. They can catch animals that are much bigger than they are.

When wolves are searching for food, they jog along at about five miles per hour. They can jog over 50 miles without resting. When they spot a meal, however, wolves put on the speed. They can run 20 miles per hour or faster.

⇐ This wolf pack is searching for food in a Montana forest.

Do Wolves Have Enemies?

Wolves do not have very many enemies in the wild. In fact, the biggest enemy to wolves is people. When we build cities and roads in areas where wolves live, we are harming these animals. Without plenty of space to run and food to eat, many wolves become sick or even die. In order to make sure there are wolves around for many years to come, we need to care for them and the places where they live.

Gray wolves like this one need large areas to run and find food. ⇒

All through history, people have misunderstood wolves. People heard wolves howl at night. They saw wolf tracks near the bodies of dead animals. People thought wolves were dangerous animals. They believed that wolves would kill anything, even people.

As you have just learned, wolves are not like they seem in scary stories. They are not mean, angry killers, and they do not eat people. Instead, wolves are smart and important animals. Perhaps if more people understood these animals, they would write more stories about how wonderful wolves really are.

⇐ Wolves like this one often like to rest in tall grasses.

Glossary

alpha (AL–fuh)
The alpha wolf is the leader of the pack. The alpha is usually the oldest male in the group.

camouflage (KAM–oo–flazh)
Camouflage is colors or patterns that help an animal hide. A wolf's fur blends in with its surroundings and acts as camouflage.

endangered (en–DANE–jerd)
When an animal is endangered, it is in danger of dying out. Red wolves are endangered.

packs (PAKS)
Wolves live in groups called packs. Packs are made up mostly of members of one wolf family.

predators (PREH-duh-torz)
Predators are animals that hunt and eat other animals for food. Wolves are predators.

pups (PUPS)
Pups are baby wolves.

Index

DATE DU

AP 11 '06	8 9
JE 2 '06	10
NO 3 '06	
NO 23 '06	
OC 85	
NO 29	
04	
00-19	
DE 16	NOV
MAR 2	